When Your Teenager Stops Talking—
How Do You Learn What's Going On?

An excerpt from
Teenagers and Parents
12 Steps to a Better Relationship
by
Dr. Roger McIntire

Summit Crossroads Press
Columbia, MD

Copyright 2016 by Roger W. McIntire

This is an excerpt from *Teenagers & Parents: 12 Steps for a Better Relationship* by Dr. Roger McIntire. The complete book may be ordered from Amazon.com and other online bookstores and wherever books are sold.

Teenagers & Parents: 12 Steps for a Better Relationship is approved by Parents' Choice Foundation.

Published by Summit Crossroads Press, Columbia, MD. USA.
Contact: sumcross@aol.com or 410-290-7058.

ISBN 9780961451967.

All rights reserved. No part of the material protected by this copyright notice may be reproduced or utilized in any form or by any means, electronic of mechanical, including photocopying, recording, or by information storage and retrieval systems without written permission from the publisher. Printed in the United States of America.

Dr. Roger McIntire is available for speaking engagements. His books provide excellent discussion material for parenting groups and may be ordered in quantity at sizeable discounts. E-mail sumcross@aol.com for more information.

Table of Contents

Listen Well (Tips for Learning What is Going On)
1. "What Are You Saying About Me?"
2. Slow Down, Use "It" Not "You" to Reduce their Stress and Yours
3. Careful when Teaching Lessons and Fixing Blame
4. Looking, Smiling and Other "Non-Verbal" Signals
5. Pass Up the "Quick Fix"
6. The Real Topic May Not Have Come Up Yet
7. Suggest Solutions with Care
8. Beware of Arguments for Entertainment's Sake

Avoid Shortcut Parenting
1. One-Ups and Put-Downs in Shortcut Parenting
2. Placing Blame and Giving Credit
3. Look for Needs Instead of Blame
4. Avoid the Temptation to Increase Blame as They Grow Up
5. "I Always Felt I was Never Quite Good Enough"

Preface

Eight to twelve-year-olds are often called "Tweens," so, I suppose, the "teenager stage" begins at about ten in the U.S. It blossoms early and develops rapidly probably because of so much adult experience—mostly second hand—from TV, CD's, mobile devices, social media.

Computer companions pass along, music, information, or misinformation, about life, sex, social skills, and almost everything else. We parents need to know what's going on and we rely on what we observe and what they tell us.

As the next ten years rush past and our teenagers choose their next adventure with college, job or life, our chances for conversation appear and disappear from one situation to the next. Your listening skills are crucial to building moments of conversation where you can learn about their struggles, provide some advice, and smooth the path through some of their troubles.

All of the theories —about siblings, birth order, genetics, and early experiences—contribute to understanding our kids, but such past influences cannot be changed. Mom's and Dad's best opportunity to influence their teenager, really their only opportunity, is confined to the here-and-now—the present family interactions.

Many counselors believe that parents who hold back too much have a lasting negative influence on their children. One counselor friend of mine works with corporate administrators who often suffer from depression. She said she often found that the root of the problem was an unfulfilled need for acceptance from their Dads. She added that every man longs for the day when his father says, "You're the son I hoped you would be."

Daughters have had the same longings, I'm sure, and Mom's acceptance is just as important as Dad's. But Dads may hold back on the gushier stuff just when it's needed most. Often called upon to be the heavies—*Wait 'till your father gets home!*—Dads may miss their opportunities to give deserved praise and admiration.

Questions and solutions raised in this book come from both parents and their teens who were clients, regular readers of my column or website visitors. Common questions from the kids were reported by parents, "Can we talk?" "Can I quit school?" "What birth control is best?" "I want a sister. You have more eggs don't you?" Parental questions range from, "How can I deal with her tantrums?" to "What about his computer addiction, her Facebook obsession and their questions about alcohol, drugs and sex?"

The struggle to grow up is a confusion of emotions mixed with a desire to break free from parental and a desire for parental admiration and support. Of course, teenagers want to be on their own and different from their parents. And conversely, parents want their children to stay close to their example and be more like them. The compromise develops gradually in a mixture of granting greater independence and decreasing control.

Listen Well
Tips for Learning What is Going On

When the question comes up, *"Mom (or Dad), can we talk?"* the answer needs to be a careful one. An answer to the let's-talk-question that leaves the choice of topic with your son or daughter *("Sure, what do you want to talk about?")* leaves the door open. An answer that takes a direction may lead your teenager astray. *"Is this about that math homework?* could sent him off --never to return to his first trouble. If you and your son or daughter have this part right, all other topics will be easier. So go slowly here and thoroughly review your conversational habits when talking with your teenager.

Listening skills don't come naturally to most of us. But, with a little practice and extra attention, the skills will help you for the rest of your parenting years.

1. "What are You Saying About Me?"

Many people, especially teens, are most interested in themselves. They tune in to the parts of conversations that are about them, and they are a little less interested in the rest. The most important part of the conversation will be, *"What are you saying about me?"* Talks with our teens can go sour immediately when we parents think our teenager's *mistakes* are the most important parts while our teens, first of all, pay attention to the implied *personal evaluation*!

Ten-year-old Kirby: *"Mom, Carlin is still texting"*
Mom: *"Carlin, no texting at the table. You're being rude."*
Carlin: (15 years old) *"Just a minute."*
Mom: *"No, now. Tell me about your soccer game."*
Carlin: (mumbling and still texting) *"Have to sign off. Kid brother just squealed."*
Mom: *"Put that cell phone away. I told you before, it's rude!"*

This moment turns into an argument because a ten-year-old was making trouble and Mom responded by adding the evaluation that Carlin is rude. When trying to set rules, leave the personal evaluation out—it changes the topic to him.

Mom was right to ignore Kirby's intention of making trouble but adding the personal evaluation of Carlin only distracts him to building a defense. Mom could have said, *"Stop texting at the table, Carlin and tell me how your game went."*

Let's give Dad a chance.
"You should have seen what happened in gym today, Dad."
"What, Donald?"

"Keith got in an argument with Mr. Effort, and they ended up in a real fight!"
"I'm sure it wasn't much of a fight."
"Yes, it was. They were wrestling!"
"I hope you didn't have anything to do with it."
"Naw, all I did was cheer."
"Cheer? Listen, Donald, you'll end up in trouble right along with Keith! Don't you have any more sense than to..."

Let's interrupt Dad here for a moment. Dad criticized Donald's story: (1) he thinks Donald exaggerated because it wasn't much of a fight, (2) he thinks Donald might have had something to do with it, and (3) he thinks Donald should not have cheered.

Dad centered the conversation on what he disliked about his son's behavior instead of the story. All this happened in a 20-second discussion. Donald, like all teens, will resent the way his dad redirected his story into a talk about his mistakes. In the future, Donald will drift further away and Dad will get less and less information.

Dad's style of continual correction puts Donald on the defensive. Donald only wanted to tell his story for the joy of it, without corrections that lead in other directions. Here's the first point of possible misunderstanding and conflict. A teen may extract a personal evaluation in less than a sentence. If the signals are negative, up come the defensive reactions before any useful exchange begins.

Let's back up and give Dad another chance to be

more friendly and yet still communicate the possible consequences of the gym-class experience to Donald.

Dad's second chance:

> *"You should have seen what happened in gym today, Dad."*
>
> *"What, Donald?"*
>
> *"Keith got in an argument with Mr. Effort, and they ended up in a real fight!"*
>
> *"How did it all start?"* (Dad ignores the possible exaggeration, doesn't express doubt, and shows interest instead.)
>
> *"They just started arguing about the exercises, and Keith wouldn't give in."*
>
> *"Hard to win against the teacher."* (Dad's comment is a general remark about teacher-student relationships and it's not critical of Donald.)
>
> *"Yeah, Keith is in big trouble."*
>
> *"Did they ever get around to the exercises?"* (Dad shows interest in the story, not just in making points and giving advice.)
>
> *"Keith was sent to the office and then we tried these safety belts for the flips. Do you know about those?"*
>
> *"I don't think we had them in my school."*
>
> *"Well, they have these ropes..."*

Donald may have a clearer view of the incident now and he may understand the hopelessness of Keith's argumentative attitude. He wasn't distracted by having to defend himself when he told Dad the story. And now he's explaining something to his father. Dad's positive evaluation of Donald comes through in his respect for him and interest in what Donald is saying.

Teens are forever on guard to protect their fragile self-confidence. Carlin is on the lookout for Mom's opinion of him and Donald is on the lookout for Dad's criticism. We parents sometimes concentrate our efforts on their mistakes, but our teens place that in second place, at best.

2. Slow Down, Use "It" Not "You" to Reduce their Stress and Yours

Deliberately slow your pace of conversation so your child-teen can slow his. Even a sassy teenager is not likely to have your way with building thoughts into words and will become defensive when he's rushed or runs out of vocabulary.

> Thirteen-year-old Marie: *"This terrorism business is awful."*
> Mom: *"Well, you just have to learn to live with it. The world is dangerous."*

An argument has already started. Of course Mom didn't mean that terrorism is not awful, she just moved on (too quickly) and made her daughter the topic instead of terrorism (You just have to learn…) and missed the opportunity to agree with her daughter.

Mom is next in line for a "Yes, but...," an exchange leading to a louder argument because her pace is too fast. Now the focus has changed to winning the argument. Mom will make her points and Marie will struggle to stay even. Distracted now by the argument, there will be little help with anxieties about terrorism. Sons and daughters in this situation copy their parent's argumentative style of conversation that only looks for mistakes to correct. A simple conversation has turned into a competition.

> Fifteen-year-old Teen: *"I've got so much homework."*
> Mom: *"Sounds like…they gave you…a lot."* (Good remark. with a slow pace, and Mom only repeats what her teen said.)
> Teen: *"How can I do all of this?"*
> Mom: *"Well, why not start with…"* (Mom stops and remembers to avoid jumping in with advice.)
> Teen: *"I'm not going to do any of it!"*

Mom starts to threaten grounding for a week if homework is not done, but she remembers to avoid punishment and instead says, *"You're really good at math, maybe you could just start there."* (Mom risks a quick-fix mistake but, mixed with the compliment about math, it's likely to be taken positively.)

Learning the "it-habit" instead of the "you-habit" can also reduce the stress of conversation by not centering the topic on your teen. When Dad gets his second chance with Donald he says, *"How did it all start?"* "It" helps avoid both the instant-evaluation-of-Donald pitfall and slows a conversation that could be going too fast. When a conversation seems threatening to your teen, try to look at the subject as an "it" instead of "you." This tactic avoids the trap of "attack, defense, and counter-attack." Conversation doesn't make a good competitive sport.

Mom: *Leave your baby brother alone, Justin.*
Justin: *I was just going to pat him.*

Mom's first impulse may be to say, "*I know what you were going to do, just stay away, you'll wake him!*" Her second impulse might be, "*I like to pat him, too. But it might wake him and he's tired.*"

Justin drops some crumbs from his potato chip bag.

Now Mom's first impulse might be to say, "*<u>You</u> are so messy! Look what you did!*"

But her second impulse might be, "*Oh, look what happened. Better pick those up before they get trampled into the carpet.*"

If Mom chooses her first impulse, she emphasizes Justin, the person. *You* will wake him, *you* are messy. If she chooses her second reaction to each event, she emphasizes a situation that *she and Justin* are dealing with together: *It* will wake him. Look *what* happened. It won't make a lot of difference to Justin on these two occasions. But over the long haul, Justin will end up with a very different message about himself and a very different relationship with Mom.

3. Careful When Teaching Lessons and Fixing Blame

The opportunities to "teach a lesson" and "fix the blame" are temptations most of us parents find hard to resist. But sometimes the benefit of getting more facts outweighs the "quick-fix" or the "make-them-sit-up-and-take-notice" approach. People who avoid instant evaluation and defuse confrontation with an objective conversation of "it" topics are easier to talk to. They are interested in the other person's experiences, not in placing blame or emphasizing mistakes.

Mom: *"How was art class today?"*

Amy: *"Oh, OK, what I saw of it."*

Mom: *"What do you mean?"*

Amy: *"Mrs. Clay sent me to the office."*

Mom: *"What did you do?"* (Attack #1)

Amy: *"I didn't do anything!"* (Defense)

Mom: *"You must have done something; you aren't sent to the office for nothing!"* (Attack #2, conversation going badly)

Amy: *"You never think it's the teacher's fault; you always blame me."* (Counter-attack, looking for a way out)

Mom: *"What kind of talk is that? Let's have the whole story."* (Attack #3, conversation almost destroyed.)

Amy: *"Oh, nuts!"* Amy stomps out. (Conversation dead)

Mom can do better by avoiding the personal evaluation by using the "it' topics.

Mom: *"How was art class today?"*

Amy: *"Oh, OK, what I saw of it."*

Mom: *"What do you mean?"*

Amy: *"Mrs. Clay sent me to the office."*

Mom: *"WHAT happened?"* (Emphasizes "it" instead of "you" IT happened. This is better than, "What did you do?")

Amy: *"Tom ripped my paper."* (The conversation takes a new turn with Amy's answer to the "it" question.)

Mom: *"Oh, no!"* (Emphasizes sympathy rather than an evaluation of the upcoming mistake.)

Amy: *"Yeah, so I shoved him."*

Mom: *"And so she sent you to the office?"* (Mom's focus is on facts and providing some sympathy instead of reprimanding something that's already been reprimanded at school.)

Amy: *"Yeah."*

Mom: *"Then what happened?"* (Good "it" question that avoids "let's get to the bottom of [your mistake in] this!")

Amy: *"Well, for one thing, I'm behind in art again."*

Mom: *"Well, if you can stay away from Tom, maybe you'll catch up. What else happened today?"* (Mom adds a little parental advice and then on to looking for something more positive)

Too often we parents begin at the wrong end of the conversation. After our teen exposes a problem or troublesome topic, we often jump to the end in order to fix the problem. In our rush, the message becomes, *"Stop talking, you're wrong, I'm right, and I'll tell you what to do."*

Effective conversational strategies take time, but if they become a habit, the rough parts of family talk can become smoother.

4. Looking, Smiling and Other "Non-Verbal" Signals

There is more to conversation than what is said and what is heard. Folding arms, getting louder, and looking away all speak volumes. Looking is particularly important. For example, watching the TV, while holding your hand over the mute button, ready to restore the sound, may irritate your son or daughter more than a yawn. A teen will quickly learn these signals and may increase his aggressive style just to regain your attention.

Smiling can also be a big factor in getting along. One marriage councilor I know said she counts the expressions of support and agreement between husband and wife. If she notes less than six per hour together, she becomes pessimistic about the relationship. However, she counts smiling as one of the positive expressions. Actually she counts every smile as two in looking for six per hour.

A slump may also show an uninterested attitude. It's best to face your conversational partner. To accept your solution your teen has to stop thinking about himself and take up the courage to admit you could be right. Knowing how seldom he is likely to reach this opinion, sit up and show interest. Most talks with your teen will not reach a conclusion. That's OK, family conversation should not be a tennis game where every ball must be returned and every game scored and posted. Let it end as it so often does with your friend at work—additional understanding and support, but no answers. *Give* a nice day.

Practice these habits with another parent or a friend while you share a simple story such as getting the kids to school or helping them with homework. Begin with one person as the listener and one as the teller. Review the following guidelines for good listening.

Keep frequent eye contact. Look at your conversation partner most of the time. A teen expects a good listener to look at him/her. We don't like to feel unattended because the person we're trying to talk with is staring at the newspaper or TV while we ask a question. Teens feel that way too.

Smile at your kids frequently. It's a sign you found something good about your children. They appreciate it.

Use good posture. Face your teen while talking and listening. Use body language that says, *"I'm alert! I'm interested!"* A parent who slumps, looks away, or even walks away sends a message that may discourage and insult the person talking.

Avoid criticism, ask questions instead. Use questions that continue the conversation by asking for longer answers than just *"yes"* or *"no."* *"How did it feel?"* is more likely to continue the talk than *"Did you feel bad?"* Emphasize *IT* questions instead of using *YOU*: *"How was it at school today?"* not *"How did you do at school today?"* Careful questions can help in a neutral, non-opinionated way, so the person asking the questions gains a better understanding of what happened and why.

Avoid solution statements and use reflective statements. Re-word the last thing your teen said to show you understand what he/she told you. *"Boy, I really hate that Mr. Jones for math!"* could be answered with, *"He really annoys you"* or *"You get mad in there a lot, I guess."*

Replace the temptation to give advice or criticize by reflecting your partner's statements instead. Suggestions such as *"Why don't you . . .?"* or *"Have you tried . . .?"* might make the story teller feel inferior, resentful, and argumentative. You will get the whole story by reflecting. Your listening helps because the speaker will clarify the situation and his feelings.

Share your experience. Share stories, jokes, and experiences that helped you learn about getting along in life. Be selective, avoid stories that are too close to a sore point with your teen. If your son or daughter feels your experiences are not directed as advice to his or her specific weaknesses, the tales can be enjoyed, and they will improve the relationship.

5. Pass Up the "Quick-Fix."

Parents love to fix things, especially quickly! Parents, particularly fathers it seems, can be too efficiency-oriented in their conversations with kids. If you told me you had trouble tying your shoe because the lace broke, would you want me to tell you how to fix it? No. As a matter of fact, it would be a bit insulting because it implies you are a complete klutz!

Jumping in with a "quick fix" is often annoying. If Mom or Dad jumps in too soon with advice, a teen may cancel his or her next topic entirely—just to avoid more correction.

Better to jump in with a positive remark first. Identify and highlight the behaviors you like. Loving a teenager is not much without liking specific behaviors also. Mom and Dad's first parenting job is to find and compliment what is likable about their kids. Even when their teen feels obligated to brush them off, compliments will improve their self-respect. Repeat as needed. Learning is a process, not a single event.

6. The Real Topic May Not Have Come Up Yet.

Parental reactions that repeat what a teen just said often result in more information from a teen. Her first remarks are usually long on feelings and short on facts. Reflective remarks may encourage her to make up the shortfall. Also, a reflective remark can be satisfying to her because it says you understand.

Keep a regular time and place for basic talking such as a long dinner time or possibly right after school while they have a snack. Don't try to fill every pause, some silence is OK. Don't meet their expectation that you always have (pushy) advice to give. If parents jump in with early advice or opinions, their reactions could be way off target.

Reflective statements say nothing new and only repeat what your teen said in different words. Without adding anything new, this agreement keeps the conversation going and provides opportunities to get straightforward information without defensiveness.

Reflective statements also require a little creativity to avoid looking simple-minded or manipulative, but in small amounts these reactions can allow teens to continue *their* topic of conversation. Let's look at an example of reflective statements in action by a mother learning about her daughter.

Amy: *"Man, is that school boring!"*

Mom: *"It's really getting you down."* (Mom is reflective and just uses different words for "you are bored")

Amy: *"You bet."*

Mom: *"What's getting you the most?"* (A good it-question starts with *"What,"* instead of, *"Why are YOU so bored?"*)

Amy: *"I don't know. I guess it's the whole thing."*

Mom: *"You need a break."* This is reflective of "the whole thing (is boring)" and is a sympathetic remark that avoids, "There must be something wrong (with you)!"

Amy: *"Yeah, but summer vacation is six weeks away."*
Mom: *"Got any plans?"* (Good, puts the conversation on a positive topic.)
Amy: *"No."*
Mom: *"Hard to think that far ahead."* (A reflective statement that just repeats "No plans" with sympathetic words)
Amy: *"Pam is looking for summer camps online."*
Mom: *"Sounds like a good idea."* Avoids the quick evaluation of, "Camp might be expensive...it might be too early to apply, etc." Immediate negative evaluations only discourage the search for answers at this early stage.
Amy: *"I might go online and look for some myself."*

A complaint about boredom is a familiar remark to most parents. Although not much is solved about boredom in this conversation, Mom has a better understanding of her daughter's feelings and has avoided the temptation to "get something done" in this short talk. Indirectly, Mom said she has had similar feelings to her daughter's, and it's all right to have those. Most important, it's all right to talk to Mom about feelings without being criticized for feeling bored.

By allowing her daughter to direct the topic, information flowed to Mom, instead of from her, and she has a "ticket of admission" for next time:

"Say, did Pam ever get any camp applications?" or,
"Only five weeks left now; how's it going?"

Notice there is no room for adding old complaints in this approach. Avoid frequent criticisms such as, *"You shouldn't be bored," "You don't plan ahead like Pam'"* or out-of-left-field complaints such as, *"You spend too much time on the computer!" "You never do your homework!"* and *"You have bad friends!"* Such criticisms are too broad and will be taken personally because they say, *"And while I'm thinking about you, another thing I don't like is..."*

Instead, encourage your teen to take the conversational lead and postpone parental topics. Later sections in this book will deal with those other complaints.

Help your teen explore alternatives. Reflecting your teen's statements can help him or her get to a point of exploring alternatives to a problem and taking action to solve it. When a parent sends the message, *"I heard you,"* and *"It's all right to feel the way you do,"* your teen is likely to go beyond letting out feelings to considering, *"What can I do about it?"*

A parent helps most by tuning in to her teen's level of feeling and energy. Is she looking for alternatives, considering a particular one, or just letting out emotion? Parents must listen with empathy and react appropriately to give support. If your teen is getting rid of emotion, a helpful parent reflects that. At other times a teen may be exploring the alternatives.

Megan: *"Those kids are always dissing me online. I don't know what to do."*

Parent: *"What alternatives are there?"*

Teens are creative at listing options when they are ready. But if no idea comes up, the problem may not be clear yet and your teen needs to explore more by expressing opinions and feelings.

Perhaps Megan is ready to try an alternative.

Megan: *"I'm going to tell those kids to quit bugging me!"*

Parent: *"How do you think they'll react to that?"*

Megan: *"They might stop, but if they don't I'll just ignore them from now on."*

Parent: *"Just ignore them?"*

Megan: *"Yeah, that works every time!"*

Well, the ignoring strategy may not work all the time, but Megan is now encouraged to take control and is working on her own problem—that's a step toward growing up.

Distinguishing different teen levels of emotion and energy and reacting with support requires practice and empathy. When in doubt resist the temptation to suggest solutions.

7. Suggest Solutions with Care.

We are always tempted to suggest solutions to our kid's problems: *"Why don't you . . ."* *"You should try..."* *"Don't be so . . ."* These statements are well intended, but they often strike the listener as pushy and superior. Most of us don't react kindly to suggested solutions that are too early.

If you told me you're frequently late for work because of traffic, and I said you should get up earlier or take another route, you might be offended. I was just trying to be efficient giving quick advice, and we often just want to fix things—preferably quickly, but efficiency in conversation is for business meetings and TV shows—not family discussions.

Family conversation should be enjoyed; it's not a job to get out of the way so we can get on to the really important stuff. Teens need time to talk to you. As one lonely teen put it to me, *"If all they want is a project, why don't they take up a hobby?"*

Your teen may have her own phone but does she still resent your phone conversations with friends? Because they take too much time from her? Possibly, she may also resent the friendly, non-efficient nature of your conversation with your friends that doesn't come through when you talk with her. As an example of overcoming the temptation to fix things too quickly, look at the following conversation:

Sarah: *"Life is so depressing. People are so bad."*
Mom: *"I know it gets like that at times."*

Here's a good start. It may seem like a terrible start because the topic is so discouraging, but that's Sarah's choice. A terrible start would be for Mom to fall to temptation and disagree with her daughter right away by trying to "set her straight" with the solution: *"You shouldn't talk like that; there are a lot of good people in the world!"*

This correction is tempting but unnecessary—Sarah knows her remark is extreme. Also, it's somewhat dishonest on Mom's part because she knows Sarah is partly right. Since the statement has some potential for agreement, Mom's reflective statement takes the side that puts her closer to Sarah. Let's see how it goes:

Sarah: *"It gets like that all the time at school."*

Mom: *"There must be some times that are good at school."*

Not good, Mom's saying, *"You're wrong,"* and it's too early in the conversation for the implied disagreement, authority, and the solution expressed in this nudge. Let's take that back and try again:

Mom: *"School's been bad lately, huh?"*

This is better because it's reflective without evaluating who's to blame; it keeps the conversation on a third entity where Sarah started it (not her fault; not Mom's). The next remark from Sarah is likely to be informative about what the problem is at school. Mom, if careful, will learn a lot and Sarah will *"get it all out."*

In most conversations between adults, the suggestions for solutions are left out completely. We don't end up a conversation with a neighbor by saying, *"So we're agreed you'll cut the hedge at least every two weeks!"* or, *"So don't go roaring off in your car like that, it disturbs everyone!"*

Be satisfied that most conversations with your teen,

like those with your neighbor, will have no immediate conclusions or results. Leave out the closing comment in most of your conversations. If you try to be the "winner" in every talk, then you will always have to make someone a "loser."

8. Beware of Arguments for Entertainment's Sake.

Is the conversation just an argument for entertainment? The answer to this is particularly important when the argument is really about what your teen says, not what she does. Intentions are not actions, but they can produce entertaining arguments. Your teen may want a reaction from you or to convince you that you can't always control her. Some of your teen's behavior in school and other places are away from your influence and that could be one reason school and other outside activities are her favorite topics.

A teen's more obnoxious stories may be re-designed for your ears alone, just to push your button or get you to argue! Most of the time, your reaction should be plain vanilla, especially regarding abstract or distant situations.

When Todd's father first talked to me, he told me about Todd's stories about rude remarks he says he made to his teachers, the stories always resulted in a sharp reprimand from Dad.

Dad's typical reaction was: *"You better watch what you say, those teachers work hard to help you and you just give them trouble!"*

Then Todd came back with: *"Dad, you don't know, they*

don't care about me, they're just in there for their paycheck!"

Then Dad countered with: *"Well, you'd better listen to them if you want a paycheck of your own someday."* The argument is a destructive one, each looking for weaknesses in the other, no winners, no progress. But there is a little entertainment for Todd.

Todd said he didn't like these arguments, but that's questionable because he always came back for more. As a matter of fact, his mother told me, *"I just don't get it. I think Todd deliberately stirs up his Dad."*

Of course, Todd didn't intend to insult his teachers. That was too dangerous. He just *talked* about insulting them, maybe to relieve frustration, or to stir up a little excitement at home, or both. Being only 14, Todd might not even know he has a habit of putting down teachers at home, and no idea *at all* as to why he does it. If Todd's parents want a change, they need to work with the behavior in front of them, not the threat of what he does, or could do, at school.

We need new topics for Todd and his dad to talk about, and they need to be worked out in advance. If Dad has some good topics in mind, he and Todd wouldn't be so easily drawn into verbal fencing matches.

With new topics and Dad on the alert for chances to compliment and encourage Todd for reasonable conversation, the family airways will improve. Some of the best habits for parents are ones that help them stay alert to see and react to the best behavior of their teens.

Reflecting a teen's statements can help move him toward exploring alternatives and taking action to solve a problem. It helps when a parent sends messages, "I heard you" and "It's all right to feel the way you do." Then your daughter or son is likely to risk talking about possible answers to questions like: "What can I do about it?" or "What would help?" A parent helps most by tuning into the teen's level of feeling and energy for the problem.

Is your teen looking for alternatives, considering a particular one, or just letting out emotion? All of these purposes are good. A parent may listen with empathy and react appropriately to give support. If her teen is just venting emotion, a helpful parent reflects that and does not give or push the teen to look for answers.

Lori: *"Mr. Factors is a terrible math teacher! He won't even let you ask a question."*

Mom: *"Questions are important in math—to get the problems straightened out before going on."* Good. Mom stays clear of who is right, Lori or Mr. Factors.

Lori: *"Sure. How can I learn if he won't answer the questions?"*

Mom: *"Does he ever review?"*

Lori: *"Oh, sure, he reviews, but it's so fast nobody knows what he's talking about."*

Mom: *"Why don't you go in after class?"* (Whoops, Mom just took a superior view here. Lori may counter with, *"That won't work"* or *"I tried that."* Let's give Mom a second chance)

Mom: *"Why does he go so fast?"*

Lori: *"Who knows? What a jerk."* (Lori's voice is lower now, running out of steam for this topic.)

Mom: *"Hmmm."* (always a good response in tricky situations.)

Lori: *"Some teachers are so hard to deal with."*

Mom: *"Hmmm, Yes."*

You may feel impatient with Mom in this conversation. Why doesn't she help? Couldn't she at least encourage Lori to go in after class? Or encourage her to speak up insistently in class?

If this is the third complaint about Mr. Factors, Mom might give some of that advice, but on the first round I think she should pass up the temptation to give advice and just let her daughter know she's on her side. How can her daughter feel comfortable and spontaneous in bringing up sensitive topics (at this age, they all seem to be sensitive) and venting some steam if Mom always takes a shortcut to a solution and "quick fix?"

Avoid Shortcut Parenting

With so much competition from TV, CD's, mobile devices, social media, Facebook, Twitter, U-Tube, talk shows and movies, chances for a talk with your teen may become precious. When the opportunity comes up, here are some reminders.

The first priority in parenting should be finding things to highlight about our kids. If Mom or Dad zero in on the shortcut of looking for the obvious mistakes, blunders and bad behavior, they may miss the gems and successes. Reprimands are easier to think of and compliments take more time. As we parents react to what our teens do, messages accumulate every day about what we like and what we don't like. If you are on the lookout for bad behaviors your messages can overwhelm the less frequent expressions of love.

This can be one reason some growing daughters and sons become alienated from the family and would rather go outside with friends or stay in their own rooms. Often it is the likelihood of criticism, "put downs," and corrections that drives them away.

A habit of saying "I love you" is not much without frequent messages that say "I like you." Finding behaviors to like is the main business of being a parent.

Your habits are contagious and your attention is the main part of the family atmosphere. If looking for mistakes become the routine, parents might not like the parenting job and look for shortcuts to shorten the time spent. The family atmosphere follows that mood. Teenagers will respond in kind, recycling the wrong attitude through the family.

Teenagers sometimes engage in a conspiracy—almost unconsciously—to convince you that you are having no effect. But don't be misled. Your influence may not show up in the short run, but your reactions do make a difference. Don't give up. Watch a certain behavior for a few weeks to test your influence and notice how upset they get when they feel ignored. Attention, praise, and general encouragement are handy rewards. They should be used often.

Vague expectations about what good behavior is and specific descriptions of bad, lead to unbalanced parental messages that say "I don't like you" more often than they say, "I like you." Bad behavior may attract most of the attention because the "good" behavior is not spelled out well enough to be easily noticed. Getting down to the specifics of good behavior leads to many advantages.

For example, parents who are alert and praise the small successes that are the parts of larger accomplishments send clear messages about behavior. The kids develop and improve with small, easy steps instead of becoming discouraged by reprimands for small mistakes.

Developing a great parent-teen relationship should be a part of every day. Teens long for the joy and safety of it; and parents take satisfaction and pride in it. Your relationship is developing from a mixture of your understanding of what's going on, your messages, rules, listening, and your example. Consistent strategies are key ingredients in cultivating this relationship.

Basic heredity and personality will still show through in a growing family, but a review of daily events can often be useful because a parent can plan to withhold reactions, and deliberately provide a positive model. The best outcome would be that we all get what we deserve and improve our behavior as a result. Of course, out in the real world of your teenager, some justice is done, but undeserved rewards do occur and satisfaction only happens to a degree.

1. One-ups and Put-downs of Shortcut Parenting.

Put-downs and one-ups disrupt useful family conversation. They give too much attention to winners and losers. Then parents have a tough time getting any information about the temptations and troubles the kids are facing.

Where does shortcut parenting lead? Both parents and teenagers may have verbal habits and attitudes that can turn an otherwise valuable conversation into an argument.

Put-downs are a tempting parenting shortcut to get

Mom's point across, but they are often too vague and personal. For example, vague complaints are sometimes triggered by a particular infraction, "Only ignorant people use that language." Of course he knows you're talking about a particular (usually four-letter) word, but, for impact, this parental objection is expressed as an insult of the whole person.

Better to avoid the general put-down and focus on the present mistake. "Don't say that word in our family; it's rude, abusive and as an adjective to "car" it doesn't even make sense. It sounds as if you don't know enough language to express yourself."

I agree this is still a put-down but, focused on the specific behavior with some extra explanation, it is more constructive. This will not immediately take care of the problem, but at least your teen may search for other words next time. When he finds them, let him know you are impressed.

One-upmanship is also a bad habit. It usually comes near the end of a conversation when we decide to declare ourselves the winner. We often like to see starts and ends where only a continuing process of change exists. For example, as parents we hope to persuade our children to avoid bad habits by not starting them. No smoking, no drugs, no alcohol.

Conclusions on the end of these conversations are better left off. "So I don't ever want to hear that you..." is better replaced by a reason, "Once those brain cells are gone, they don't re-grow."

These discussions will continue beyond the age of 20. The best help will be your example and your reasoning against the bad habits. Statistically, smoking kids come from smoking families. Alcohol abuse breeds alcohol abuse—regardless of Mom's and Dad's rationalizations or excuses for their own behavior. Teens copy better than they listen.

Here's another example.

Dad: *"You can't quit school. You won't get anywhere without an education."*

Teen: *"They don't teach anything I need to know."*

Now Dad could remain inflexible, stay with put-downs and disagree, saying his son needs to learn the basics and doesn't know what needs to be learned.

He could also go with a one-up. *"Your mother wouldn't have the job she has today if she had quit, and I wouldn't be teaching without my extra schooling."*

A better approach might be to look for agreement. Certainly there's more to learn since we were in school. Maybe he is right about what he needs to know, and it's time to look to the school for a better menu. Just working out what else needs to be learned may help him start learning it, whether the school decides to teach it or not.

All candidates for public office know it's dangerous to admit they are not perfect, right, efficient, and the best. But candidate strategies are not productive in family conversation.

Parents can easily slip into office-candidate modes with their own children, but unlike political campaigns where only the candidates are judged, at home everyone is in for the long haul and everyone is a player on stage. This makes a big difference.

Conversation should not be a game. In games, for every winner, we imply there is also a loser. If parents play to win, the games will be short because parents have more practice putting everything into words. Sooner or later Mom and Dad will not be able to find a "loser" who wants to play.

"How was school?"
"Same old thing."

Mom has a choice right away. She could say, *"Come on, something must have happened."* Mom's score is up one, daughter's is down one. Or Mom could leave the score at zero saying, *"Gets pretty dull in the middle of the year."*

"Yeah, everybody's going nuts having to stay inside all day—even for soccer practice."

Now Mom could say something else agreeable and understanding, *"This weather has certainly been awful."* Or she could play to win, *"Well, at least you have more time to get your homework done."* Mom's score is up one but her daughter's alarm goes off. Here comes Mom's favorite topic and criticism. Her daughter's defenses are activated. Parents can easily slip into this shortcut mode. One Mom told me, *"I don't have all day to blabber; she needs to spend more time on her work, so I have to steer her in the right direction when I have the chance."* This is a parenting style reserved for speaking to children, of course. We know the conversation will end soon, and we want to wrap it up with our point.

Better to forget about the ending and let most conversations explore situations without conclusions. Neither side wants instructions anyway.

A disadvantage to adversarial games with children is that losers quickly become non-risk takers. Then creativity goes down and conversations increasingly become defensive and short. Sometimes both sides end up just attacking and defending.

Often parents suspect that these confrontations have become a habit and an entertainment. They are inefficient encounters for a teen looking for the satisfaction of dominating at least in a conversation at home.

You don't have to be drawn into these tennis-game conversations. It isn't necessary to return every argument with a retort. Take your time with reactions as you would with an adult. Just, *"Hmmm"* or *"Ahhh"* is often enough. Avoid the personal comments as much as possible and encourage your offspring to think (and talk) like an adult.

With the time-limit ignored and the score left at zero, future talks will be frequent, more productive and probably more interesting.

Parenting shortcuts often come up short. They can make us feel we are protecting and disciplining our kids when we are actually giving no specific help or instructions at all.

"You need to try a little harder to be nice at these family gatherings."

"Your manners were terrible, and you should be nicer to your cousins."

"You had better shape up and make an effort, Jeff."

Mom's well-intended advice to Jeff is of little help. Trying harder, showing better manners, being nicer, shaping up and making an effort are not specific. They could strike a teenager as magical ideas.

These general directions leave enough loopholes to allow Jeff to avoid any new effort and still have room to defend himself later. Better to be specific and say, *"When your aunt asks you about school, stop and answer her."* Better yet, *"Stop and tell her about your science project."* The specific suggestion is no longer magical, and if Jeff takes the advice, he can be more pleasant next time.

Sometimes we engage in magic to avoid direct confrontation and sometimes because we have no answers. We only know we want things to be better. One Dad said to me, *"He knows what I mean. I don't have to spell it out for him."* Vague criticism makes it easy for Dad but it is confusing for a teen.

"Jeff, you had better start acting right."
"What did I do?"

"You're always fighting with your sister."
"She starts it."
"Well, you'd better learn to get along."

Not much information in this exchange. What is "acting right?" What strategy should Jeff learn to "get along" besides the one he has already selected—blame the problems on his sister?

Better to quit this game of teen-parent dodge ball and be specific, *"Jeff, when your sister calls you names, tell her you won't talk to her when she does that and then leave."* Will this advice solve the problem? Probably not, but a specific plan gives Jeff a little more control and Dad a way to be truly helpful.

Separating sister and brother is sometimes necessary but doesn't teach much. It just satisfies Dad (or Mom) with a temporary stop to the arguing. Dad's guilt is relieved because he has "done something" about the problem.

Often it's our definitions, or lack of them, that get us into trouble. *"OK, you can ride your motorbike out on the road, but be careful."* What does "be careful" mean? Go slow? The whole idea of getting on the road is to go faster. These two are going to have another argument about the motorbike. Mom should be specific or refuse to let him use the road.

To make real progress, Mom will need to identify the actions of her son that will directly contribute to a better adjustment. Usually this requires coming up with specific and clear alternatives to bad behavior.

The best advice you can give your teenagers is not spoken but shown. Your example is the best control you have in arguments. If you lower your voice they will lower theirs, and you'll have a better chance to get your suggestions across to them.

Girls and boys need any encouragement we can give, and the most useful encouragement will be your time—time for listening, time for talking over career plans and time for looking into the prospects after high school graduation. Don't be discouraged by a teenager's apparent lack of enthusiasm for these topics. Kids often feel obligated to act independent (I don't need any homework help) and competent (I know all about those college programs).

It's a parenting pitfall to become discouraged by the apparently indifferent attitude of a teen and leave him or her short on helpful conversation about these topics.

When your school asks for volunteers for field trips or away games, encourage Dad to take on the opportunity. It will give him a chance to learn more about his children, and it will set a standard for students who need the male example.

In those conversations at home, remember that often a teenager's number one fear is embarrassment. Avoid beginning with a question you know they can't answer, *"How are you going to learn if you don't pay attention?"* Start with information they might want, *"Here's a flyer on that golf scholarship in Virginia. What do you think? Maybe we should drive down and take a look."*

Don't be too busy for mealtime talk. Mealtimes can provide a snapshot of general family happiness, but many families have given up the tradition. Breakfast is either nonexistent or taken on the run in the morning rush. Lunch takes place at either school or work. Shawn eats by herself in the evening also, in front of the TV. Her big sister snacks and sends text messages to friends. Dad and Mom eat supper while watching the news. Little time is left for serious talk.

Without mealtime practice, parents and kids forget how to talk to each other. Family conversation is reduced to sound bites. Parents try to get in their points and the kids mimic the latest patter from TV sitcoms where zingers have been memorized in advance. Big mistakes can result.

Mealtime talk is often replaced by other rushed conversations designed for a purpose. Joey at 15 years old can talk at a breakneck speed if he thinks talking fast and acting impatient will get an "OK" when a slower pace might produce a "no."

Joey: *"Dad, Ross and his family are going to the school football game tonight. Can I go?"*

Dad, still looking at his e-mails: *"Ah, what did your mother say?"*

Joey: *"She said it's up to you."*

Dad, still looking at his computer: *"OK, as long as you*

are with them."

With more mealtime practice Dad might have recognized Joey's devious use of "family" and said, *"Who did you say was going?"*

Joey might have said (still in the rapid fire mode) *"Ross and some of his family."*

And then with a very painful face, *"Dad, he's waiting on the phone."*

'Dad, knowing Joey's impatience, might have said, *"Let's talk it over. Do you mean Ross's brother is driving?"*
Joey would say, *"Dad, I don't know who all is going. Anyway, Ross's brother is a good driver, can I go or not?"*

A teenager's view is on the short-term, but Dad should have paid attention to more than going to the ballgame. Certainly Joey's idea of what makes Ross's brother a good driver is not enough.

Dad missed all this and while the consequences were serious, they were not tragic. Ross's brother was arrested for driving under the influence, and it caused a family row. Dad said Joey had mislead him, Joey said he hadn't. Little was said about drinking and driving.

Are you too busy for a slow pace? Most of our social habits are learned from our parents' example and will not be learned by the kids if we are too busy to sit down and take time with supper. *"They've got to learn to shift for themselves,"* one Mom told me. What choices will they make and who will teach them to "shift for themselves?"

Sit down with the kids for at least one meal every day—deliberately use a slow pace, no newspaper, no TV, no mobile devices. This is a great time for family stories. Avoid starting remarks with "you," don't try to steer the conversation, don't try to "win" and, oh yes, don't expect changes in the first month.

The crucial question confronting parents is not whether rewards, punishments, encouragements, and discouragements will be used to influence a teen's behavior. In day-to-day living that influence is inevitable. The question is whether parents will have time enough to plan some of these consequences so that their teen will be encouraged to learn what needs to be learned while growing up.

The emphasis on the defects in the person will act as a punishment. Jovial and approachable people never seem to punish. They seem to have a rule that says, *"When mistakes happen, emphasize <u>outside</u> events."* To the extent that we must correct, contradict, reprimand, and punish, we risk losing this friendly air.

Selecting behaviors for positive attention is the main business of being a parent. Your habit will be contagious and the whole family atmosphere will be more positive.

If looking for mistakes becomes the routine, parents may become unpleasant and they may not like themselves when doing the parenting job. A teenager will respond in kind and avoid the family situation when possible.

Parents and their sons and daughters should be

friends. Not in the sense of enjoying the same music or having friends in common, but through enjoying time together and supporting the strengths and successes of each other.

Friends bring out the best in me. When we meet, their attention sweeps the common ground between us looking for sparkles to highlight. I like the "me" they draw out. I return the compliment, like a friendly searchlight, seeking the best in them.

Some people have another focus. Their search overlooks the good in me and zeros in on vulnerable spots. I pull back and risk very little. I know what they're looking for. I cover up.

Aim *your* searchlight carefully. What are you looking for?

2. Who Deserves the Blame and Who Deserves the Credit?

Positive communication promotes more comfortable and informative conversations. But through the processing and maneuvering in a family, it may go beyond conversation to the complex negotiations of parenting. This development creates dangers in placing blame and giving credit in parent-teen negotiations.

We usually give credit for successes, but for mistakes and failure, we distribute the blame in one of two ways: For *our own* mistakes we usually choose "outside blame" that finds the explanation in circumstances outside of ourselves. This makes us unfortunate victims of situations outside of us, *"It was so noisy in there, how could anyone think or be able to do the right thing?"* "Outside blame" also includes people, *"I was too distracted because people were coming so late!"*

When it comes to the mistakes of *other people,* we are tempted to use "inside blame." *"What (inside condition) makes him so inconsiderate, so clumsy? Why doesn't she pay more attention? What was she thinking of?"*

Inside blame is a dangerous parental habit. It leads parents to frustration because their teen is viewed as "having" (inside) an almost unchangeable character.

Outside blame leads parents to look for problem *situations* instead of problem *kids*. With a good understanding of a problem situation, you have a chance to support a workable solution, and that, in turn, gives your teenager a new chance. In order to plan reactions to problem situations, a parent needs a clear view of what's happening. Blaming your teen doesn't help because it makes assumptions about what is going on inside.

Nick: *"Dad, can you drive me to soccer practice now?"*
Dad: *"Just a minute, Nicholas, I'm listening to your mother."*
Nick: *"Oh great, if I'm late for practice, I won't get to play on Saturday."*
Dad: *"Just a minute!"*
Nick: *"We need to leave right now!"*

Dad: *"A minute ago you were watching TV, now we have to drop everything and rush".*

Nick: *"Forget it. I just won't go."*

Dad: *"You just said ..."*

Nick: *"I mean, I'll just skip Saturday, too."*

Dad: *"Just get in the car, OK?"*

Nick: *"OK, if you insist."*

Dad: *"What!?"*

Later, Dad says: *"Nick is so selfish. He sits around watching TV, then demands immediate service because he's late! And then, he blames me for insisting he hurry! His switching the blame drives me crazy!"*

Mom: *"Maybe he is selfish, but we could try a rule that says all rides require a 5-minute warning before take-off time. And any time he tries abusing us like that we should just say, Well if you really don't mind not going, OK!"*

Dad: *"You're right. Soccer is less important than giving him the message he can't twist us around like that."*

Mom: *"It might not always come out perfect, but at least we will take back a little control of the situation."*

Instead of fixing the blame inside Nick (he's selfish), Mom suggested they try changing their reactions to Nicholas when he makes a demand. It could be he's doing it for attention and even an argument about his demanding nature could be rewarding.

The complaint that Nicholas is *"too demanding and selfish"* refers to real actions of Nicholas, but also implies the problem is part of his nature. The result is that the blame has been put inside Nicholas, and his parents may believe that any change can only come from there.

The *"Why?"* of a teen's behavior is best answered by changing *"Why?"* to *"What happens next?"* Nicholas makes an inconsiderate demand and then what happens? His ride comes through *and* any disruption is blamed on Dad for not cooperating on demand. What different consequence could be planned? The answer is not always simple and obvious, but Mom starts at the right place by looking for a solution instead of blaming Nicholas. This approach is more productive than giving up and just labeling him "selfish." The new focus may lead to a plan to support Nick's considerate behavior and to exercise caution in reacting to his little traps.

Parents can be on the lookout to give credit for the good accomplishments of their son (or daughter), but they often feel these opportunities are few and far between. The problem may be partly due to the way behaviors are described. If good behaviors are only vaguely defined, they are less likely to occur and be recognized. Deciding just when to support a teenager may not be easy:

Matt (age 13): *"I got my room cleaned up."*
Dad: *"Great!"*
Matt: *"I didn't pick up the parts to my model because I'm not finished with it yet"*

Here's a crucial moment for Dad. His choices are: continue support for what was done; after all, half a loaf is better than none, or hold out for a higher standard and only give credit when the whole job, with the model put away, is done and the credit is due.

A definition of what is acceptable would help; doesn't Matt have the option of leaving one on-going project out? Matt's parents will have to make this judgment of Matt's progress and potential, but the parental habit here should be to err to the side of encouragement—there are few circumstances in adult-rearing where there is a danger of an overdose of support.

Another concern for Dad is what kind of credit should he give? "Outside credit" may be "no credit" (support) at all for Matt: *"I guess the mess finally got to you. Even you couldn't stand it any more."*

So Dad may give the credit to Matt's environment for driving Matt to do the right thing, But also, Dad shouldn't take the credit himself by saying, *"Well now, didn't I tell you that would be better?"* Dad should send the credit directly to Matt for getting the job done:

Dad: *"Well, you still need the model out; you would have to just about wreck it to put it away. You* (not me, and not other influences) *have it looking really good in here!"*

3. Look for Needs and Instead of Blames

Recognizing the priorities of needs can sometimes explain the otherwise puzzling fate of some rules. For example, I worked with two very different sisters whose reactions to cleaning up their rooms were very confusing.

Michelle needed to be constantly assured that her parents thought she was capable and successful, and she tried hard to be cooperative and helpful. Her sister Susan, also seemed to value her parents' approval but wanted prolonged attention and companionship more than praise.

A rule that reminded their mother to praise both daughters for keeping their rooms nice worked well for Michelle seeking confirmation of a job well done. Since attention ended when the rooms were done, attention-seeking Susan procrastinated in doing her part just to keep the cleaning going on and on. Susan prolonged the room-cleaning chores for the attention she received—even negative attention would do—while our more goal-directed Michelle worked hard for the confirmation of her success.

Mom may want her daughters to clean up their rooms to keep the place looking nice, but does she have to be right on top of them while they do it? The reason may be that while she thinks having a nice room is the point of the clean-up (a long-term goal), the daughters' priorities may be quite short-term—one wants assurance that she is contributing (doing it right); the other wants attention for doing any work at all!

Mom has *two* strategies to work on. One strategy Mom carries out deliberately—encourage them when they clean their rooms; the other strategy is an unintentional one of giving unusual attention to Susan's procrastination. So Susan *slows up* for attention, but Michelle *finishes up* for praise.

The solution for Michelle and Susan's mother came with the insight that Susan needed attention at the end and long after the chores were completed. This attention did not need to be in the form of praise for room-cleaning; it just needed to continue in order to show Susan that finishing the room didn't finish Mom's attention.

It would be a mistake to conclude that Michelle wants to please Mom and Susan doesn't. Or that Susan just wants to aggravate her mother. These conjectures about sinister Susan would only lead to more nagging and a sour turn in Mom's relationship with Susan. Mom is the adult and *she* has to make the special effort, after room-cleaning, to show interest in Susan.

4. **The Temptation to Increase the Blame as They Grow Up.**

As children become teens, blaming them is increasingly tempting for parents, *"They're old enough to know better!"* This habit can distract parents from looking for a chance to give personal credit when it is deserved. For example, you might know a teenager who is moody, disrespectful, rebellious, or cynical. This might be a "long-standing habit" (inside blame) and his parents may think, *"That's just the way he has always been."* But even older teens act the way they do partly because of the way they expect to be treated—because of what has ordinarily happened next.

Teens may be disrespectful because the only time they are taken seriously is when they act disrespectful, or their bad behavior may produce an entertaining argument, or their bad talk may seem more "adult" than saying something pleasant. Even some adults believe that!

When a disrespectful teen turns happy and cheerful, adults may pat him on the head and tell him he's a "nice boy" but otherwise ignore him. The usefulness of bad behavior in this situation is not lost on a grumpy teen.

Showing respect for your teen by asking for his opinion, showing confidence in his abilities, and doing a good job of listening will bring out an improved form of respect in return. This strategy, an example to be modeled, encourages an attitude that will replace "disrespectful."

Dad: *"It's too early for a garden outside, but we could start seeds inside. What do you think, Nick?"*

Nick: *"What good would that do?"*

Dad: *"Later, when you plant them outside, they would have a head start."*

Nick: *"Even melons and stuff like that?"*

Dad: *"Even melons. Let's do melons."*

5. "I Always Felt I Was Not Quite Good Enough."

Many parents have told me that while they were growing up, their parents always pointed out the room for improvement. *"I always felt I was not quite good enough,"* was one father's comment to me while telling me he wrote a letter to his mother every week throughout his adult years until she died. But each letter was criticized for leaving out some detail. "I wish she had just once said that she appreciated all the news; she never wrote me, she always called and pointed out some person or subject that had been left out of my latest letter."

It is a shame that many never experience such deserved appreciation. But the greater tragedy is that while a parent holds back compliments, the kids become discouraged with the task and resentment sets in. It takes courage to overcome the disadvantage of parents who have been too stingy with their compliments.

A parent's short-term job is child-rearing, but the long-term goal is adult-rearing. To reach that goal, children need examples of how adults handle their responsibilities and how they talk.

The purpose of this short book is to point out conversational habits that can encourage your teen to keep you informed about what is going on in their sometimes dangerous world.

At the same time, you are also the dominate example in your teenager's world of how to be a grown up. How you talk and how you listen will, is, and has been copied. Your words are their model even when you are in disagreement.

Of course, you have to be comfortable in your own home and cannot be forever watching all that you say, but when your kids take up their own topics, be thoughtful. Let them explore their topic, <u>practice</u> their topic. Don't "change the subject" by changing the focus to their behavior. Even when they are 20-something, they are watching and listening.

<u>Give</u> a nice day.

www.ingramcontent.com/pod-product-compliance
Lightning Source LLC
Chambersburg PA
CBHW070100020526
44112CB00034B/2120